6:45
Music &

The Heart of
CHRISTMAS

Blk Pants

God's Greatest Gift
Our Greatest Choice

A Musical Created by MIKE SPECK

Arranged by Mike Speck, Cliff Duren and Danny Zaloudik

Orchestrated by Danny Zaloudik

lillenas
PUBLISHING COMPANY

lillenas.com

Contents

Emmanuel

Words and Music by
JOHN DARIN ROWSEY
Arranged by Mike Speck
Cliff Duren and Danny Zaloudik

PLEASE NOTE: Copying of this product is NOT covered by CCLI licenses. For CCLI information call 1-800-234-2446.

way in a man - ger a long time a - go, on a ho - ly si - lent night, the mid - night was clear on that first_ no - el, as the an - gels were heard up - on high. His en - trance was not one of

8

robe and a crown — should have graced the new King, but He came as the low - ly of men. Still, shep-herds and wise men knew He was Mes - si - ah; the

CD: 6

a - tion sings Em - man - u - el!   Em -

man - u - el,   sing hal - le - lu - jah! Em - man - u - el,   re -

demp - tion is come.   Em - man - u - el,   shout ho - san - na,

12

NARRATOR: *(without music)* God with us...what a thought! God, the architect, ruler and sustainer of all Creation...*(music begins)* choosing to become one of us...choosing to come to earth with the heartbeat of a baby.

King of Eternity

with
What Child Is This?
Hark! the Herald Angels Sing

Words and Music by
SQUIRE PARSONS
Arranged by Mike Speck
Cliff Duren and Danny Zaloudik

16

20

NARRATOR: *(without music)* Christ, the King chose to leave His throne to come to earth...choosing to become one of us. The story of Christmas is a story about choices. We are going to discover that every person who took part in the wondrous event we call Christmas was faced with choices... beginning with God. *(music begins)* For God Himself chose the perfect moment in time and the precise location for the birth of the Savior. He chose a common teenage girl to be the mother of His Son. I wonder how many of us have ever pondered or considered the dilemma of this young Jewish girl, named Mary, the one God had chosen? She was engaged and waiting for her wedding day when an angel appeared to announce that God had selected her to bear His Son. Although God had chosen Mary, would she submit to the will of her Lord? You see, God would never force Mary to do something contrary to her will. For God gave mankind, from the beginning of time, the freedom of choice. Would she choose to obey God or would she run away? Would she tell Joseph, her fiancé, of her glorious blessing, or would she hide in shame? What would her parents think? What would her friends think? Surely she realized the consequences, yet she still chose to surrender to the Lord's marvelous plan for her life. "Be it unto me according to your word" was Mary's choice.

I Will Be Your Servant

Words and Music by
REBECCA PECK
Arranged by Mike Speck,
Cliff Duren and Danny Zaloudik

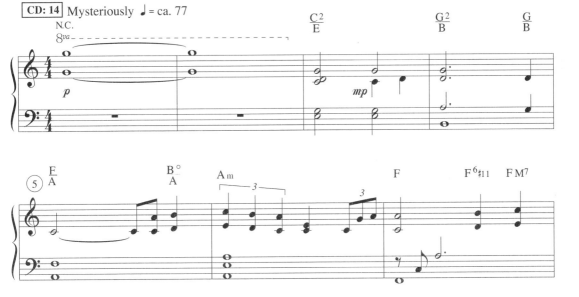

22

CD: 15

Solo (Mary)
mp

The road a -

F6/9 G9sus G9 G9sus

32

head will not__ be eas - y. The task be - fore me seems__ so__ great.__

Fm6/C C2 F2/A

36

____ Lord, I don't know why You__ would choose__ me, but I will

C/G F2 G/F Em7 Am7

CD: 16   40

trust You and__ o - bey.__ I will be__ Your serv -

F/Bb F2/A Gsus G C2

- ant, Lord,— I choose to do— Your will.

*NARRATOR: The Lord does all things well and what He does, He does perfectly and completely. Just as God chose Mary, He had also chosen Joseph to be the earthly father to His heavenly Son. Now Joseph was a just man...and after hearing of a coming child, not wanting to disgrace Mary, he decided to secretly break the engagement. But God intervened and sent the angel of the Lord to Joseph in a dream and told him the Child that Mary was carrying was conceived in her by the Holy Spirit. Joseph pushed back his fear and chose to obey the voice of God and took Mary as his wife.

26

29

30

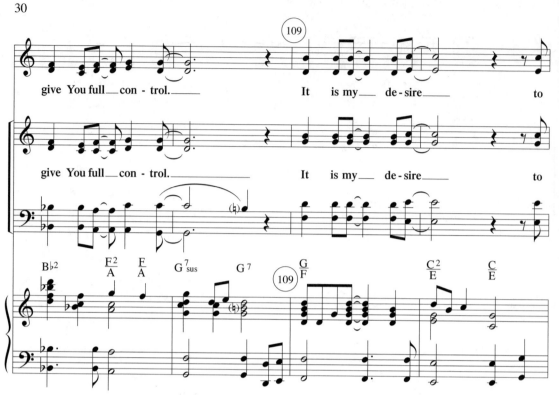

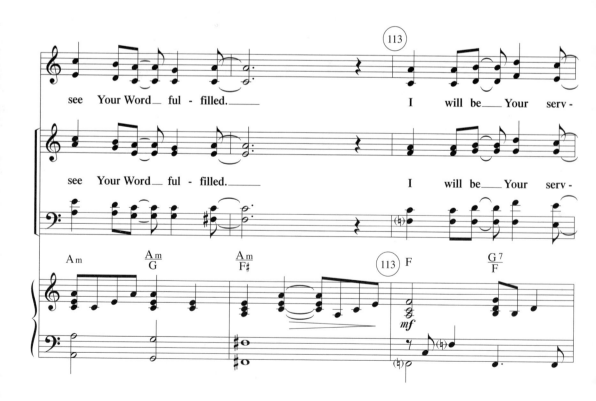

NARRATOR: *(without music)* And Mary brought forth her first-born Son, and wrapped Him in swaddling clothes *(music begins)* and suddenly a multitude of the heavenly host began praising God and saying, "Glory to God in the highest and on earth peace, good will toward men!"

So Much God

with

Angels We Have Heard on High
Glory to God in the Highest
The Birthday of a King

Words and Music by
CRAIG EDWARDS
Arranged by Mike Speck,
Cliff Duren and Danny Zaloudik

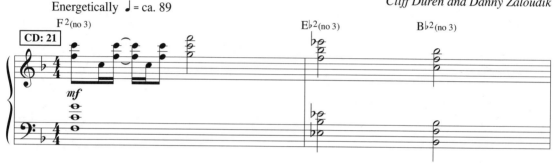

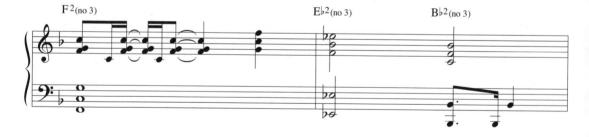

PLEASE NOTE: Copying of this product is NOT covered by CCLI licenses. For CCLI information call 1-800-234-2446.

Christ the Lord, the new - born King.

*"Glory to God in the Highest"

Glo - ry to God in the high-est. Peace on earth__ and good will to men. Heav-en-ly an-

Choir: 2nd time only

Glo - ry to God in the high-est. Peace, good will to men.

-gels an-nounced His ar-riv - al in___ the lit - tle

An - gels an-nounced His ar-riv - al

G♭   E♭m

town of Beth-le-hem. Hal - le - lu - jah to the Lord, sing ho - ly. He was born___

in the town of Beth - le - hem. Hal - le - lu - jah, sing it.

A♭7   D♭7   (29) G♭

CD: 24 1st time

—to save the world_from sin. Glo-ry to God in the high-est. Glo-ry, hal-le-lu-

He will save from sin. Glo - ry to God, hal-le-lu-

Gb   Ebm

32

- jah to the Lord. A - men!

- jah to the Lord. A -

1.   (to pg. 35, meas. 25)

32 Gb/Db   Db7   1. Gb   N.C.   (to pg. 35, meas. 25)

CD: 25

men! Glo-ry to God in the high-est. Glo-ry, hal - le - lu - jah, hal-le-

men! Glo - ry to God! O, hal-le-

*"The Birthday of a King"

lu - jah!

lu - jah! Al-le - lu - ia! O how the an - gels sang. Al-le-

more relaxed

CD: 26

lu - ia! How it rang!

cresc.

Em   A⁷   D   E♭⁷   E♭⁹

Trio
43 ff

Glo - ry to God in the high - est. Peace on earth___ and good will to men. Heav-en-ly an-

ff

Glo - ry to God in the high - est. Peace, good will to men.

ff

43 A♭

ff

- gels an - nounced His ar - riv - al in____ the lit - tle

An - gels an - nounced His ar - riv - al

Ab

Fm

town of Beth - le - hem. Hal - le-lu - jah to the Lord, sing ho - ly. He was born___

in the town of Beth - le - hem. Hal - le - lu - jah, sing it.

Bb7

Eb7

(47) Ab

42

-jah to the Lord, sing ho - ly. He was born__ to save the world__ from sin. Glo - ry to

Hal - le - lu - jah, sing it. He will save from sin.

A♭

God in the high - est, glo - ry,_____ hal - le -

Glo - ry, glo - ry,_____ hal - le -

A♭   E♭/G   Fm   E♭/G Fm/A♭ Cm⁷ Fm   D♭

lu - jah to the Lord. A - men!

lu - jah to the Lord. A - men!

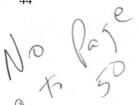

Born in Bethlehem

with

Angels We Have Heard on High

Words and Music by
RANDY VADER
Arranged by Mike Speck,
Cliff Duren and Danny Zaloudik

Children enter as music begins

With a Caribbean feel ♩ = ca. 120

*"Angels We Have Heard on High"
Choir and Congregation

45

46

48

New Kid in Town

Words and Music by
DON COOK, CURLY PUTMAN
and KEITH WHILEY
Arranged by Mike Speck,
Cliff Duren and Danny Zaloudik

*NARRATOR: Shepherds, simple men with humble hearts, were filled with fear when the angel of the Lord and the glory of His presence lit up the sky that first Christmas. The angel revealed to them that a Savior had been born. Leaving their flock and their responsibility, the shepherds hurriedly traveled to Bethlehem to find this Baby who was Christ the Lord...and there He was...lying in a manger, just as the angel had said. Scriptures reveal that they could not contain what they saw and what they heard. It's amazing that common keepers of sheep were the first to be invited to see the Savior of the world. Think what the shepherds would have missed had they chosen to disregard God's invitation.

We are not certain of the exact time, but we do know that men of great wisdom, from a distant country saw a brilliant star. Leaving houses and lands, they chose to follow that majestic star, wherever it would lead, no matter how long the journey might be. What would cause these men to follow a star? Why would they spend a portion of their life and their own money, looking for a King of another kingdom?

These honorable men searched diligently...bearing gifts of gold, frankincense and myrrh... they were determined to find the young King and to worship Him.

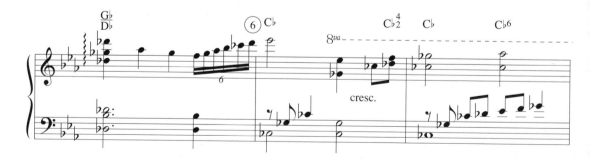

51

CD: 35

Men *mf*

We're

F   G/F   F   G/F   Gm9/C

30

look-ing for the King,_____ the new Mes - si - ah.

F2   Bb2   F

mf

34

We're fol-low-ing the star_____ shin - ing

F   F2

38

bright - er._____ Please, man, won't you

Bb2   F   C2   Dm7   F2/C

CD: 36

help us if you can? He shook his head___ and point-ed his hand.___ There's a

B♭2   F/A   G m7   C 2(no 3)

42

mf

new Kid in town,___   *Choir*   and I   *(mel.)*

42 F2   F2/C   F

think He's just a few___ doors down the road.___   *No*   There's a

A m7   B♭2   B♭   F   F2/C

54

here in Beth - le - hem.

*Narration continues

*NARRATOR: Sometimes we fail to consider the human side of this story. The star that led the wise men brought them first to the city of Jerusalem. It's not surprising that these learned men went through official channels in their search for the Messiah. They questioned Herod, the governor of Judea, as to the whereabouts of this new King. He had to consult the chief priests and scribes to learn that the ancient scrolls had prophesied Bethlehem, a small village just five miles from Jerusalem, as the place where Christ, the Messiah would be born. I can imagine as these men entered this town of prophecy, they probably stopped someone and inquired where the King might be found... Yet those who lived within the very town did not know the Son of God was in their midst.

say you've trav-eled far, bear - ing trea - sure.

58

but un - til now there has - n't been_____ one. But there's a

cresc.

Ah_____

There's a
mf

G m7

D m / C

C

(87) Solo continues with men

mf

new Kid in town,____

and I

(mel.)

(87) F 2

F / C

F 2

F

mf

60

Love Came Gently

Words and Music by
MARTY FUNDERBURK
Arranged by Mike Speck,
Cliff Duren and Danny Zaloudik

Love came gen - tly, soft as a ba - by, born to a low - ly vir - gin girl. Wrapped in rags and laid in a man - ger,

PLEASE NOTE: Copying of this product is NOT covered by CCLI licenses. For CCLI information call 1-800-234-2446.

CD: 41

64

65

NARRATOR: *(without music)* The love that came gently that night in Bethlehem changed the world forever. This One who was prophesied by the ancients, proclaimed by the angels, praised by the shepherds and pursued by wise men, He is Savior, Redeemer, Lord and King... and the angel told Mary *(music begins)* to call His name Jesus.

Call Him Jesus

with
Jesus, O What a Wonderful Child

Words and Music by
REBECCA PECK
Arranged by Mike Speck,
Cliff Duren and Danny Zaloudik

The proph-ets told it long—— be - fore,——

PLEASE NOTE: Copying of this product is NOT covered by CCLI licenses. For CCLI information call 1-800-234-2446.

68

74

CD: 49

Glo-ry, glo-ry, glo-ry to the new - born___ King.___

Je-sus! Je-sus!

*Narration continues

Count in 2

*NARRATOR: Thou shalt call His name Jesus...for He shall save His people from their sins...
He shall be great and of His kingdom there shall be no end...He shall be called Wonderful,
Counselor, The Mighty God, The Prince of Peace!

Je-sus! Je-sus! Je-sus! Je-sus! Call Him

Choir St

The Heart of Christmas

Words and Music by
MIKE SPECK, CLIFF DUREN, LARI GOSS,
CAROLYN CROSS and NILES BOROP
*Arranged by Mike Speck,
Cliff Duren and Danny Zaloudik*

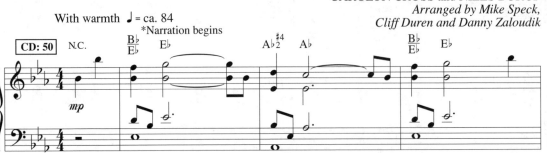

*NARRATOR: For the next few days, all around the world, people will celebrate this holiday season in some form or fashion. Many of them not really understanding why this time of year is so...alive...so anticipated...why it touches our emotions. What is Christmas? What is at the heart of it all? Let me ask you...what is the most memorable Christmas that comes to your mind? As a child, what was the best gift you ever received? Was it a certain baby doll or maybe a brand new bicycle or a wagon...some toy or favorite game? For you adults, was it something sparkly that went on your finger? Maybe it was in the driveway, with a big bow on the windshield. There are some of you older folks that remember when families weren't as financially blessed as they are today. It was a treat to get an apple, a couple of oranges...maybe some walnuts or pecans. Others of you would say the best Christmas you can ever remember was when the family was all together...in the same house...under the same roof...and life was simple. How easy it is in the day we live to miss the heart of Christmas. All the collected memories, the celebrating, the feasting...our most precious and favorite gifts cannot compare to the gift that laid in a manger on Christmas morn. You see, the heart of Christmas is Jesus... God's gift...the gift that is beyond what you and I could ever comprehend...the greatest gift of all time...for it is the gift of eternal life. The heart of Christmas is the heart of God Himself...God reaching down from heaven to love...to redeem mankind...For God so loved the world that He gave His Son that we would not perish but have everlasting life. *Stand 7*

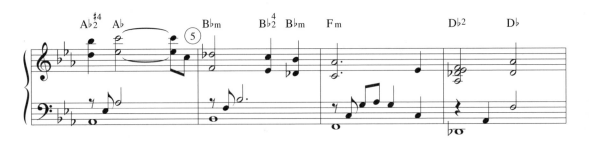

The heart of

Christ - mas, what hope it brings;_____ The

prom - ise of re - deem - ing love thro' Christ, the in - fant

King._____ So un - de - serv - ing,

yet still I find_____ God's

80

82

I Choose Jesus

with
I Have Decided to Follow Jesus

Words and Music by
ROBERT STERLING
Arranged by Mike Speck,
Cliff Duren and Danny Zaloudik

*NARRATOR: God's greatest gift can be yours and it can be mine. Each of us must choose what we will do with the gift God extends to us.

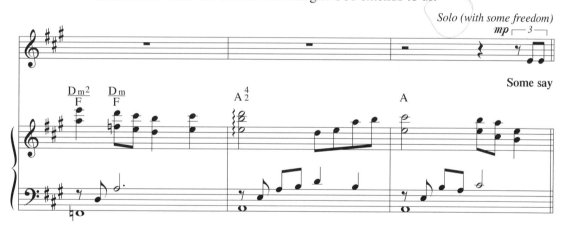

*"I Have Decided to Follow Jesus"

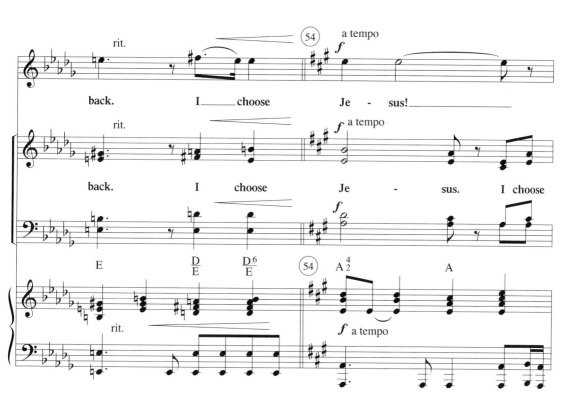

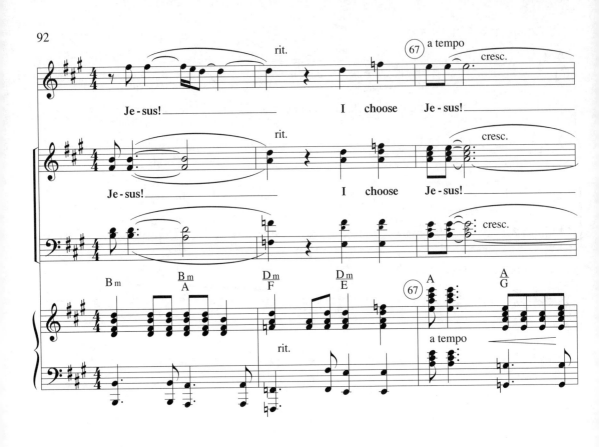

NARRATOR: *(without music)* You know, many of us chose to follow Jesus years ago and have worshipped this King for many Christmases. Christmas calls us to remember that a Savior came to give us life. It calls us to remember Mary's complete surrender, Joseph's willing heart, the shepherd's' blind faith, the wise men's determination to worship... Christmas calls to the followers of Jesus to remember our commitment and our need to give the Lord first place in our lives...and yes, *(music begins)* Christmas calls us to remember the sweet and precious memories surrounding this time of year.

Till We Remember

Words and Music by
MARTY FUNDERBURK and
TWILA McBRIDE-LaBRIDE
Arranged by Mike Speck,
Cliff Duren and Danny Zaloudik

PLEASE NOTE: Copying of this product is NOT covered by CCLI licenses. For CCLI information call 1-800-234-2446.

94

feel-ing this_ day gives_ us;_ in our

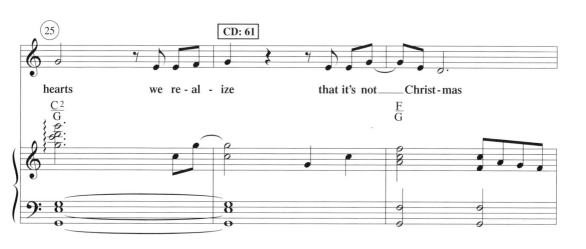

hearts we re-al-ize that it's not_Christ-mas

Choir
Solo continues

Un - til we gath - er 'round_ that old_ pi - a - no,

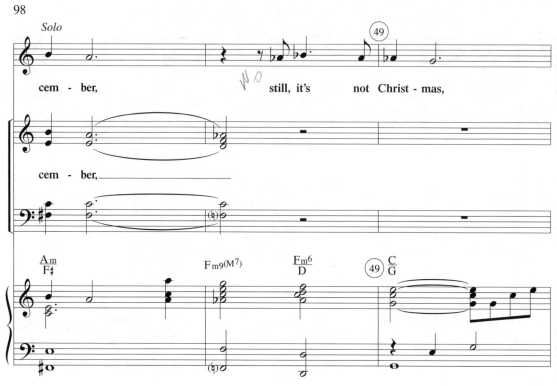

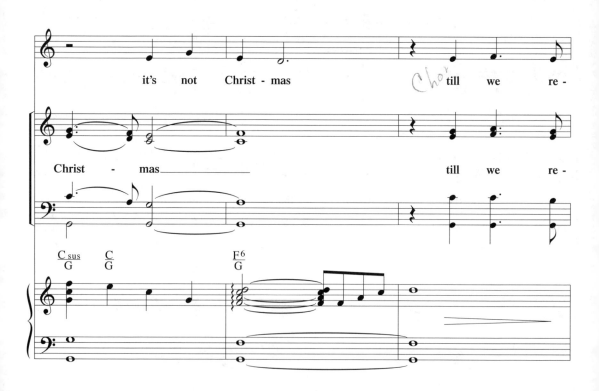

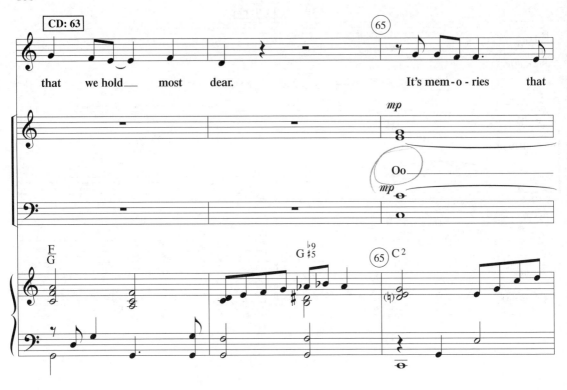

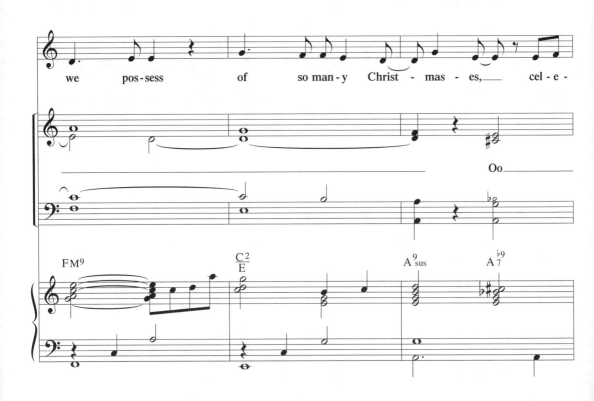

102

104

105 *Solo continues*
a tempo

gath - er 'round___ that old___ pi - a - no, sing - ing songs___ of joy___

105 D♭2   D♭   E♭m4⁷   D♭2/F   D♭/F

f a tempo

109

___ a - gain.___ O___ what a ho - ly night,___ shar - ing

B♭⁹sus   B♭7♭⁹   109 E♭m⁷

113

smiles by can - dle - light.___ And then we read that old___ fa - mil-

G♭6/A♭   A♭⁷   G♭6/A♭   113 D♭2   D♭

108

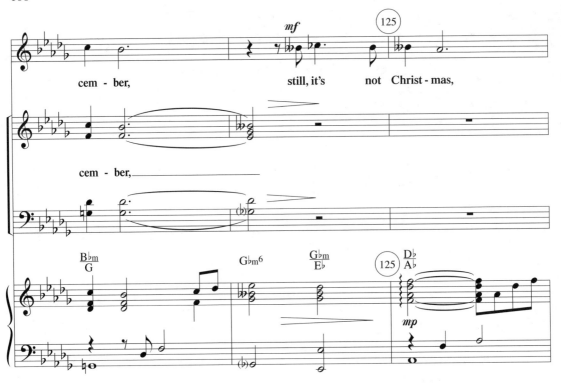

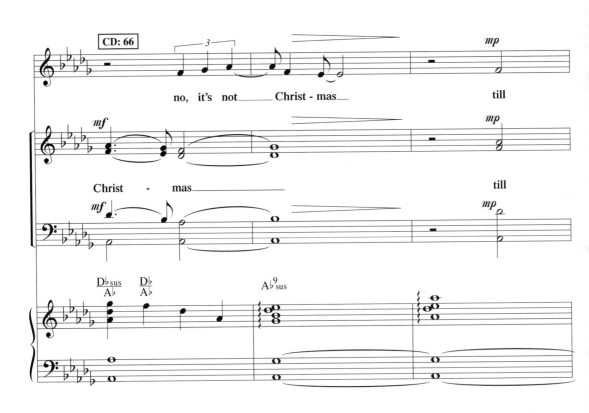

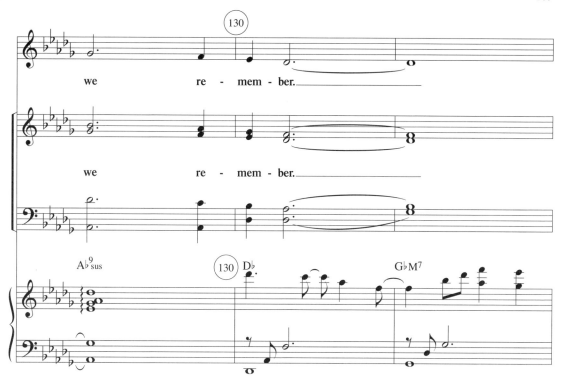

we re - mem - ber.

we re - mem - ber.

Oo.

NARRATOR: *(without music)* The heart of Christmas is Jesus...*(music begins)*
God's greatest gift...We are here to celebrate His birth for we have made
our choice...to worship, honor, and serve this Savior who is Christ the Lord!

Finale

Sing Hallelujah
Emmanuel
Glory to God in the Highest
The Heart of Christmas
I Choose Jesus
Jesus, O What a Wonderful Child

*Arranged by Mike Speck,
Cliff Duren and Danny Zaloudik*

*"Sing Hallelujah"

Sing hal - le - lu - jah,__ the Lord is__ come.__

He is Mes - si - ah,__ the Prom - ised__ One.__

Our great Re - deem - er__ is Christ the__ Son.__ Come

116

117

*"Glory to God in the Highest"

119

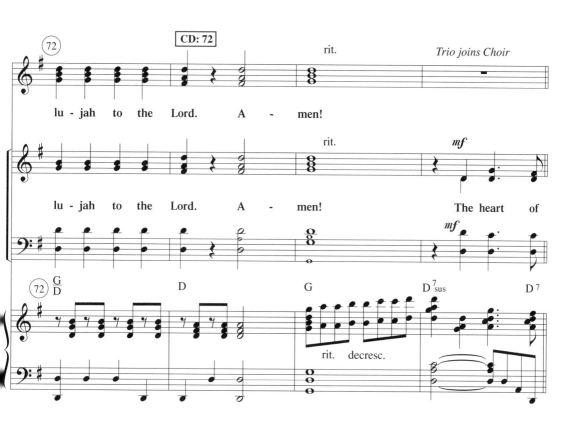

122

76 *"The Heart of Christmas"
Slower ♩ = ca. 84

Christ - mas, what hope it brings;

The prom - ise of re - deem - ing love thro'

Christ, the in - fant King. So un - de-

*"I Choose Jesus"

but for lov - ing_____ me;

Not for mir-a-cles, lov - ing me;

E♭M⁷ D⁷sus D⁷/F♯

Not just for Beth-le-hem,___ but for Cal - va - ry;

Ah_____ Cal - va - ry;

Gm² Gm B♭/F Gm/E E♭m⁶

130

Production Notes

"The Heart of Christmas" is a musical about choices. It is our prayer that this will be a tool that God can use to call all of us to "choose Jesus" each day of our lives.

The musical is driven primarily by the choir, but there are several opportunities for staging scenes during narration and song. One narrator is indicated, but two or more can be used by splitting up the lines. There are also times when the congregation participates through singing, as well as an opportunity for a pastor to offer an invitational.

Although you can stage the nativity early on in the musical, it heightens the dramatic effect if you wait until the finale. Several scenes leading up to a nativity staging are outlined below.

Place the NARRATOR on one side of the stage in front of the choir. The musical begins with the joyous song, *Emmanuel*, sung by the choir. Stage lights are bright. House lights may be up to 50 percent or more.

During *King of Eternity…*, project the lyrics to *Hark! the Herald Angels Sing* to encourage congregational singing.

The narration that follows introduces MARY and JOSEPH. It is best if the actors can sing the solos for *I Will Be Your Servant*, but you can use soloists from the choir. During underscore and narration, MARY enters and takes her place. If your actress isn't singing the solo, be sure to have some stage business for her. For instance, she can be weaving some cloth or making a basket. You may even want reenact the angel delivering the message to her. After hearing the angel's words, she can kneel and pray.

JOSEPH should enter during the narration after the first verse and chorus. Place him on the opposite side of the stage from MARY. Again, if your actor will not be singing the solo, have stage business going on during the duet portion. Keep MARY and JOSEPH apart and don't have them acknowledge each other until the choir joins in on the chorus after the duet. Then have the two meet center stage to talk to each other or to finish the song depending on whether you have chosen to use them as soloists.

Born in Bethlehem… is led by the choir and provides opportunity for a Children's Choir to sing. The chorus of *Angels We Have Heard on High* provides a place for congregational participation as the children's choir enters. This is a quick transition, so be sure to rehearse the entrance and exit of the kids several times. If possible, place the children down center in front of the adult choir.

On the narration before *New Kid in Town*, when the line "…men of great wisdom…" begins, the WISE MEN enter from the back of the sanctuary. Loosely following the lyrics, the story points can be played out as they "journey" to Bethlehem. Verse one: along the way, they meet a MAN and ask him for information, but the MAN doesn't know where they need to go and points them in another direction.

Then during the second narration, the WISE MEN meet with HEROD and his SCRIBES to confirm that they need to go to Bethlehem. Once in Bethlehem, they meet another MAN who while singing the solo of Verse 2, tells them where to find the baby and then leads them off and out of the sanctuary after the chorus. Lights go to blackout at the end of the song.

As the music for *Love Came Gently* begins, lights come up very slowly on a scene of MARY and JOSEPH with the baby JESUS. This can be staged center stage or to the left or right. The new parents take JESUS out of the manger. They hold Him, and talk together about Him as the choir sings. Beginning with one or two people, the choir lights candles and holds those during the song to represent the light that Jesus' birth brought to earth. This can also be done with the congregation.

Lights fade out slowly with the last remaining light on JESUS going to blackout by the end of the song. MARY and JOSEPH exit with the baby during blackout and the candles are extinguished.

Bright stage lights are brought up during narration before *Call Him Jesus….* House lights may also be brought up to 50 percent or more. After the song, lights fade on the choir and house lights go to black. Special on NARRATOR is up.

As the narrator quotes John 3:16, the lights are brought up on choir and they sing, *The Heart of Christmas*. Slides are projected to encourage congregational singing. House lights stay down during the song.

During the introduction and narration to *I Choose Jesus…*, lights go down on choir. Stage lights illuminate the NARRATOR and soloist. During *I Have Decided to Follow Jesus*, the house lights can be brought up to 50 percent or more. At measure 54, a banner is brought down the center aisle with the name "Jesus" on it. It is carried to center stage to face the audience. As the song ends, the lights fade slowly with a focus only on the banner and then quickly to a blackout.

At this point in the musical, the pastor may give a short message and an invitational. During the invitation strains of *I Have Decided to Follow Jesus* can be played on the piano.

The narrator continues with the introduction to *Till We Remember*. Lights should be down in the house with focus on the narrator.

During the song *Till We Remember*, a modern-day family Christmas gathering is played out. If possible, stage this near your piano or have your piano brought downstage for part of the scene. A decorated Christmas tree, some gifts, and a couple of chairs make for a simple set. At the beginning of the song a GRANDMOTHER and GRANDFATHER enter and put the finishing touches on the tree.

As they finish, their grown DAUGHTER, HUSBAND and GRANDCHILDREN come to visit. They greet each other with hugs and smiles. Then they all settle in so that the kids can open a gift or two and listen to GRANDPA read the Christmas story. During the second chorus, they all gather around the piano and pantomime playing it and singing together. As the song ends, the family holds each other's hands and they pray together. After the song, the lights go blackout and the family exits the stage.

As the final narration starts, lights are brought up on the NARRATOR. Lighting for the *Finale* should be bright and cheerful. The *Finale* is a great time to stage the nativity. If possible, keep the stable set hidden until this point. The set can be brought out during the blackout after *Till We Remember*. Be sure MARY, JOSEPH and baby JESUS are in place before lights are brought up on the set.

Visitors such as the SHEPHERDS come to the stable during the finale. You can also have the MEN from *New Kid in Town* and the WISE MEN come to the stable even though this happens later in the biblical account. Be as simple or elaborate as you wish. You can suggest a stable by using two rough wooden stools and a manger, or you can build a small barn. A star can be hung above the stable, and ANGELS can be gathered at higher points in your choir loft or staging areas. You can also use live animals. Do what works best for your church.

The nativity scene also provides a nice backdrop for your audience as they leave, and they can visit the scene before exiting the sanctuary.

As you've read through these notes, you can see that the musical offers a lot of flexibility as you tell the traditional Christmas story. We hope that you will make this musical your own as you use it to minister to your congregation and community.

Production notes were adapted in part from the premiere of "The Heart of Christmas" performed by Mims Baptist Church, Conroe, TX under the direction of Kevin Kendrick.

FOR INFORMATION AND BOOKINGS CONTACT:

Mike Speck Ministries

P. O. Box 2609

Lebanon, TN 37088

(615) 449-1888